Series Life is a Business and a Jungle.

HOW TO CHOOSE A BUSINESS IDEA?

Criteria for Choosing a Business Idea and Making Money with It

Carlos Cárdenas Verde

First edition: September, 2023

© Carlos Cárdenas Verde, 2023

Cover and collection design: CG Publicidad Diseño y Soluciones Web

http://cgpublicidad.web.ve/

All rights reserved. No part of this work may be reproduced, stored in a retrieval system, or transmitted in any form or by any means (electronic, mechanical, photocopying, recording, or otherwise) without the prior written permission of the copyright holder. Infringement of these rights may constitute a criminal offense against intellectual property.

This book is designed to provide information and motivation for our readers. It is sold with the understanding that the author does not engage in the provision of psychological, legal, or any other type of professional advice. The content of each chapter is the sole expression and opinion of its author. There is no express or implied warranty by the choice of the editor or the author included in any of the contents of this volume.

Neither the editor nor the individual author shall be liable for physical, psychological, emotional, financial, or business damages, including, without exclusion of others, special, incidental, consequential, or other damages.

CONTENTS

INTRODUCTION 7
CHAPTER I: DISCOVERING YOUR IDEAL BUSINESS 9
    UNDERSTANDING YOURSELF 10
    DETERMINING YOUR IDEAL BUSINESS 13
CHAPTER II: DISCOVERING YOUR IDEAL BUSINESS TYPE 15
    HABITS TO FOSTER ENTREPRENEURIAL SPIRIT: 17
        1. *Cultivate Gratitude:* 17
        2. *Prioritize Physical, Emotional, and Mental Health:* 17
        3. *Set Goals and Objectives:* 17
        4. *Plan Your Daily Activities:* 17
CHAPTER III: UNCOVERING YOUR PASSIONS AND STRENGTHS 19
    WHAT ARE THE HALLMARKS OF A PRODUCTIVE INDIVIDUAL? 21
        1. *Organization:* 21
        2. *Focus:* 22
        3. *Health Maintenance:* 22
        4. *Simplicity:* 22
CHAPTER IV: SELECTING A PROFITABLE BUSINESS 23
    CLASSIFICATION OF COMPANIES 23
        a) *Service Companies:* 23
        b) *Industrial or Manufacturing Companies:* 23
        c) *Commercial Companies:* 23
    CHOOSING YOUR BUSINESS IDEA 24
        1. *Brainstorm:* 24
        2. *Analyze Your Ideas:* 24
        3. *Problem-Solving:* 24
        4. *Utilize Your Expertise:* 25
        5. *Market Research:* 25
        6. *Resource Assessment:* 25
        7. *Start Small and Grow:* 25
    BUSINESS MODEL CANVAS 25
        1. *Market Segments:* 26
        2. *Value Proposition:* 26
        3. *Customer Relationships:* 26
        4. *Channels:* 26

- 5. Key Partners: 26
- 6. Key Activities: 26
- 7. Key Resources: 27
- 8. Cost Structure: 27
- 9. Sources of Revenue: 27

LEVERAGING BUSINESS EXPERTS 27

CHAPTER V: CHOOSE A BUSINESS THAT GETS YOU CLOSER TO YOUR DREAMS 29

DEFINING YOUR DREAMS 29
ALIGNING YOUR BUSINESS WITH YOUR DREAMS 30
- 1. Generating Passive Income: 30
- 2. Meeting a Unique Need: 30
- 3. Creating Jobs: 30

EXAMPLE SCENARIO: CULINARY BUSINESS AND WORLD TRAVEL DREAM 30
ACHIEVING YOUR DREAMS 31
- 1. Focus on Your Dream: 31
- 2. Document Your Dream: 31
- 3. Share Your Dream: 31
- 4. Persistence is Key: 32
- 5. Set Smaller Goals: 32
- 6. Help Others: 32

CONCLUSIONS 33

ABOUT THE AUTHOR 35

INTRODUCTION

In today's rapidly changing world, the business landscape has undergone a profound transformation. The emergence of the COVID-19 pandemic forced us to reevaluate traditional work paradigms and seek alternative ways of earning a living. For many, this meant transitioning to remote work, often with longer hours, while others sadly faced the loss of their primary source of income.

These unprecedented circumstances prompted individuals to explore new avenues for income generation, ones that offered greater satisfaction and autonomy. Hours of contemplation led to a critical decision: to break free from economic dependence and embark on the journey toward financial freedom through entrepreneurship. The desire to own a business aligned with one's passions became a driving force.

However, once the decision to start a business is made, questions inevitably arise: What type of venture should I pursue? What constitutes the ideal business for me? This book is here to help you evaluate potential business ideas comprehensively.

We will delve into a profound personal analysis, tapping into our unique abilities and skills. Through the exploration of four critical factors, we will guide you in selecting the most suitable business—one that not only aligns with your interests but is also financially viable, leading you toward the realization of your dreams.

"How to Choose a Business Idea?" offers essential guidelines to channel your entrepreneurial aspirations. The journey may seem daunting, especially for newcomers, but it's also incredibly rewarding. The lessons within this book will provide you with fresh perspectives and consider aspects you may not have contemplated before. By the time you finish reading, you will have a clearer understanding of entrepreneurship and how to discover the perfect business for you—a venture that brings both fulfillment and happiness.

As you embark on this journey, questions will naturally arise. Rest assured this book will equip you with the knowledge needed to navigate the entrepreneurial landscape confidently, helping you find a business where you can work and find true happiness.

CHAPTER I: *Discovering Your Ideal Business*

In today's world, the concept of business has evolved significantly. The impact of the COVID-19 pandemic has triggered a collective shift away from conventional employment, prompting many to explore alternative means of sustaining themselves. Some found themselves adapting to remote work, often with longer hours, while others faced the loss of their primary income source.

These transformations have kindled a desire among individuals to seek more satisfying and self-directed ways of earning a living. The prospect of pursuing entrepreneurship, driven either by increased profitability or sheer enjoyment, has become a tantalizing option. Yet, the most daunting question remains: What business venture would truly satisfy you? Which idea holds the most potential, both financially and personally? Such uncertainties can obscure your vision, even if you are resolute about embarking on an entrepreneurial journey towards success.

So, how does one go about selecting the ideal business? The answer may seem simple but profound: it hinges on who you truly are. In essence, the perfect business for you is one that maximizes your skills, ignites your motivation, proves financially lucrative, and aligns with your desired lifestyle. These four guiding principles act as your compass, steering you toward the path that leads to your most fitting entrepreneurial endeavor.

In the first book of the series, "The World is a Business and a Jungle," titled "I Want to Be a Successful Entrepreneur[1]," there is guidance on self-exploration to identify your abilities and attitudes. In this chapter, we will delve deeper into comprehending these four critical aspects. As you progress through this journey, you will not only gain a better understanding of yourself but also a clearer direction in choosing and nurturing your own business. Get ready; we are about to embark on a profound journey of self-discovery.

Understanding Yourself

The concept of self-awareness is a fascinating subject, and while there is a wealth of information available on the internet about it, our aim here is not to create a psychological profile. Instead, we will provide you with guidelines to begin or enhance your journey of self-discovery. The process can be time-consuming, not only due to the extensive self-analysis involved but also because it demands impartiality. You will simultaneously be both the researcher and the subject, and distinguishing between these roles can be challenging, potentially influencing the results.

Some readers may already have a clear understanding of themselves and may not feel the need for further introspection. These individuals likely possess a high level of self-acceptance and self-worth, indicating a satisfying life to some degree. They are more inclined to explore deeper aspects of themselves. However, if this does not resonate

---

[1] You can find this book on the same platform where you got this one

with you, do not despair. The path to self-discovery is neither swift nor straightforward, but the sooner you begin, the closer you get to knowing your true self.

From the moment we are born, others begin forming opinions about us, but you cannot control these external perceptions. To embark on the journey of self-discovery, you must first disentangle yourself from the perceptions that others hold and begin examining yourself from within.

You might be wondering, "How do I know if I truly understand myself? How can I gauge the depth of my self-awareness?" Here are some telltale signs to consider:

1. Seeking External Validation: If you frequently seek validation for your opinions or feelings from others rather than trusting your own thoughts and emotions, it suggests a lack of self-confidence. Remember that your feelings and opinions are valid, and you should trust them.

2. Dependency on Others' Approval: Relying on someone else's approval for every decision, especially someone you perceive as superior or powerful can indicate a lack of self-knowledge. Seeking a second opinion is natural, but overdependence on others' judgments can hinder your personal growth.

3. Insecurity in Decision-Making: Changing your mind after initially saying yes or no, especially due to uncertainty, signifies a lack of confidence in your own decision-making abilities. Self-assurance allows you to make decisions and stand by them.

4. <u>Hypersensitivity to Criticism:</u> Reacting strongly or impulsively to criticism or mockery may indicate hypersensitivity to others' comments. Self-awareness and control enable you to handle criticism more gracefully.

5. <u>Comparison to Others:</u> Constantly comparing yourself to others and striving to be like someone else can lead you away from your true self. Embrace your uniqueness and avoid trying to become someone you're not.

To further explore your self-awareness, let's assess how you behave in four primary aspects of daily life: (see Figure N° 1)

With family and close Friends	In your work Environment
In High-Stress Situations	Thinking about Future Projects

Figure N° 1. How I am when I am...

a) <u>With Family and Close Friends:</u> Consider your reactions and interactions when you're with your family and closest friends. What brings you joy? What irritates you? These responses reveal the impression you leave on those around you.

b) <u>In Your Work Environment:</u> Analyze your relationships and reactions in your workplace. How you communicate, inspire others, and handle daily situations can provide insights into your impact on colleagues.

c) <u>In High-Stress Situations:</u> Reflect on how you react in stressful, challenging situations. Stress often reveals our true selves, showcasing qualities such as decisiveness, calmness, or impulsivity.

d) <u>Thinking About Future Projects:</u> Review your past projects, aspirations, and goals. How you envisioned your future self in those moments offers clues about your identity.

By examining these aspects, you can better understand your essence. This information is invaluable as it deepens your self-awareness and self-appreciation. Few people dedicate time to such introspection, but through this process, you'll gain a clearer perception of yourself and the value you bring to the world. You cannot deceive yourself; every experience has shaped you into the person you are today.

Determining Your Ideal Business

To identify your perfect business, we will explore four aspects:

1. <u>Habits and Daily Activities:</u> We'll start by examining your habits and daily routines. Your preferences in how you carry out everyday tasks can provide insights into suitable business ideas.

2. <u>Skills and Experiences:</u> Next, we'll consider the activities you enjoy based on your skills and experiences. Identifying areas where you excel and find fulfillment is crucial.

3. <u>Passions and Productivity:</u> We'll delve into your passions and areas where you are genuinely productive. A business aligned with your interests and profitability is the ultimate goal.

4. <u>Profitability and Long-Term Goals:</u> We'll also evaluate different business types and their profitability potential. Ensuring your chosen venture aligns with your long-term objectives is essential.

While we begin with your strongest interests, it doesn't mean that other pursuits should be disregarded. As you progress, you can explore opportunities in various fields that spark your curiosity or offer lucrative prospects. The key is to start with what resonates with you most profoundly.

With this framework, we can navigate the path toward finding the perfect business for you. The journey begins with self-discovery and leads to a venture that encapsulates your essence and aspirations.

CHAPTER II: Discovering Your Ideal Business Type

As we embark on the quest to find the right business, an array of questions invariably arises. We scrutinize ourselves, striving to discern the type of business that suits us best. Which path should we tread? Will it be lucrative? Will it align perfectly with our aspirations, or will it merely suffice? Doubts multiply, confusion sets in, and a pervasive sense of uncertainty envelops us. Understand that this uncertainty doesn't stem from fear or insecurity; it arises because the world of business offers myriad possibilities, leaving you unsure about the most suitable one. Fear not, for we shall delve deeper into this subject.

One of the pivotal factors that play a significant role in establishing a robust work routine is our habits. Habits encompass any behavior that becomes an automatic, regularly repeated action, requiring minimal to no conscious thought, and they are learned behaviors. Throughout our lives, each of us shapes our identity, constructs our lifestyle, and forms our system of beliefs and values through these habits. They define our approach to life and our role in society.

Habits are actions that we perform automatically without requiring active thought or consideration, such as brushing our teeth after every meal or looking both ways before crossing the street. Now, you might wonder how this relates to finding the ideal business for you. The answer is surprisingly straightforward. If you choose a business venture that harmonizes with your existing habits, especially the good ones, integrating it into your daily routine won't be an arduous adjustment. Instead, it will seamlessly meld into your established routines, allowing you to execute it automatically. For instance, if you have the habit of waking up early, initiating a morning-oriented business would be a natural fit for you.

Conversely, there are also "bad habits," which are repetitive behaviors that we perform automatically but have detrimental effects on our well-being or create mental barriers that hinder personal growth. These bad habits often intersect with our attitudes.

When we engage in introspection, we can identify these detrimental habits and work towards replacing them with positive ones. What constitutes these detrimental habits? They include addictions that harm our health, such as excessive drinking, smoking, and consumption of stimulants, staying up late, neglecting basic hygiene practices, and more.

A fitting quote for this context goes: "To achieve what you've never had; you must do what you've never done." The message is clear: to effect the necessary changes for this new phase in our lives, we must take action. Now that we recognize the habits that need alteration, what new habits should we cultivate to fortify our entrepreneurial spirit? Here are some examples:

Habits to Foster Entrepreneurial Spirit:

1. <u>Cultivate Gratitude:</u> Commence your day with a sense of gratitude, acknowledging the opportunity to add another page to the book of your life. Starting your daily routine with this perspective encourages you to focus on the positive aspects of each day, fueling you with the energy and motivation to progress.
2. <u>Prioritize Physical, Emotional, and Mental Health:</u> Recognize that your body is a temple that houses your most valuable "Fixed Assets." Taking diligent care of your physical health by avoiding unnecessary wear and tear is crucial. A positive attitude reduces vulnerability to illness and feelings of decline. A healthy mind keeps you grounded, in touch with reality, and equipped to navigate challenges. Sufficient sleep is an essential component of this practice.
3. <u>Set Goals and Objectives:</u> Establishing goals and objectives compels you to formulate plans for their attainment. By defining short-, medium-, and long-term goals, you create structure and devise strategies to achieve them. Prioritizing and scheduling these objectives based on their importance or time requirements is paramount.
4. <u>Plan Your Daily Activities:</u> Breaking your goals into daily tasks streamlines your path to success. It prevents you from becoming scattered and directs your focus to the necessary actions. Planning these activities, the day before ensures that you enter your workday with a clear agenda aligned with your goals.

Initiate the process of developing positive habits gradually. When attempting to establish a new habit, it is advisable to introduce it incrementally. This approach allows you to engage with it in a manageable capacity each day, facilitating its transformation into a solid habit over time. For instance, if you are incorporating exercise into your routine, you can commence with a 15-minute daily walk and gradually extend the duration or intensity. This progression, from walking to jogging or running, is a seamless transition.

Some experts suggest that it takes just over 20 days to solidify a habit. By harnessing the power of positive habits, you can seamlessly integrate them into your entrepreneurial routine. Entrepreneurship inherently encompasses various activities because each idea you bring to fruition is unique, bearing its own characteristics. However, with the right habits, these activities evolve into routines. Through practice, you can transform these routines into second nature, freeing your mind to concentrate on what truly matters.

CHAPTER III: *Uncovering Your Passions and Strengths*

A common question that often plagues our thoughts is, "What are we naturally good at?" Each person is endowed with innate abilities, some of which develop during childhood, while others stem from our deepest passions. Yet, we may not always have a crystal-clear understanding of our talents or might not even recognize them. Here, I offer guidance to assist you in discovering your strengths and passions.

First and foremost, take stock of the activities that genuinely bring you joy. Over the course of your life, you've likely dabbled in various undertakings and discovered that you excel in some while others remain less of a forte. For instance, certain individuals find delight in logical analysis, relishing challenges that involve numbers. Others thrive in the realm of visual arts, demonstrating prowess in drawing and painting, while some shine in physical activities and sports. The crucial aspect here is to pinpoint these activities and discern what it is about them that resonates with you profoundly, and what satisfaction they offer during engagement. The answers you uncover will not only indicate the degree of expertise you possess but also unveil the depth of fulfillment they bring.

Furthermore, it is essential to explore all your interests, irrespective of the time you can allocate to them. The key lies in experimentation and the pursuit of diverse endeavors.

Through these explorations, you may stumble upon an activity that profoundly resonates with you, igniting a passion that propels you forward for the sheer joy and satisfaction it imparts.

Another method involves compiling a record of significant activities you've engaged in throughout your life, especially those that left a lasting impression. For instance, if you've organized a cultural event, delve into the experience of leading people, planning events, coordinating with guests and authorities – every facet of the process. Reflect on whether these experiences brought you enjoyment and satisfaction. Alternatively, consider your involvement in athletic events. Explore the dynamics of participating in a delegation, the training regimen, the competitive aspect, the rules governing competitions, interactions with fellow athletes, and so forth.

This introspective approach helps you identify the activities that resonate deeply with you, igniting passion and revealing areas of excellence. You might discover a knack for effective communication, an enjoyment of public speaking, a talent for teaching, a penchant for sharing experiences, or a desire to make a meaningful impact and influence others.

Experience plays a pivotal role in shaping your perspective on various activities and specific situations. It enriches your understanding of the areas or ventures you wish to pursue. With every lesson applied, experience is gained. Successes and failures alike contribute to your expertise, ultimately rendering you a specialist in that domain. Your outlook will evolve, distinguishing you from others.

On the flip side, it is equally important to consider your personality traits. Occasionally, not everything we enjoy aligns with our true calling. This disconnect may arise due to either a lack of necessary skills to excel in an activity or because we harbor a deeper passion for something else. For instance, you might possess an affinity for dancing, showcasing impeccable rhythm and technique. Yet, you may not harbor the same level of passion or flair for it as you do for cooking. Preparing delectable dishes flows effortlessly from you, evoking a sense of effortlessness. When your guests savor the meal and express their delight, you derive immense satisfaction. In both cases, you exhibit proficiency, but in one, your passion and dedication shine more brightly.

This is where your focus should gravitate – toward that which ignites a deeper sense of satisfaction and fulfillment.

George Elton Mayo's renowned quote resonates deeply with this theme: "A happy worker is a productive worker." The crux of the matter is this – we are inherently more productive when we derive joy and satisfaction from a task. Tasks performed with joy tend to be completed punctually, often surpassing expectations. Engaging in activities you find enjoyable also imbues your endeavors with greater significance and imbues you with a sense of purpose.

What are the hallmarks of a productive individual?

1. Organization: A productive person can meticulously list tasks, assign priorities, and establish daily goals.

2. <u>Focus:</u> They concentrate their attention on the task at hand, tackle one task at a time, and maintain order in their work.
3. <u>Health Maintenance:</u> Prioritizing physical, emotional, and mental health is paramount. This includes obtaining adequate sleep, consuming nutritious foods, engaging in regular physical activity, and practicing deep-breathing exercises.
4. <u>Simplicity:</u> Productivity thrives on simplicity. Efficient individuals don't just do everything; they do the right things. Simplification reduces the number of tasks, optimizing time usage.

Furthermore, the ability to assess and manage risk is a critical facet. Embracing risk does not equate to recklessness or impulsive actions. Instead, it entails the calculated evaluation of potential risks and potential setbacks, ensuring they do not unduly disrupt your overall planning. Risk, in this context, denotes the calculated bet that a particular action will yield specific benefits. This calculated gamble acknowledges the potential for loss but does not permit it to profoundly affect your overarching strategy.

By delving into these facets of your persona, you can more precisely ascertain what brings you the greatest joy and where your natural talents lie. Armed with this self-knowledge, you stand poised to proceed confidently in the pursuit of selecting the perfect business venture tailored to your unique strengths and passions.

CHAPTER IV: Selecting a Profitable Business

Now that we've explored your personal attributes and interests, it's time to address the burning question: "What business should I start?" This is a common question for aspiring entrepreneurs, and it often comes with a degree of uncertainty. Let's dive into how you can make an informed decision.

Classification of Companies

Before we delve into the process of choosing a business, it's essential to understand the types of companies based on their economic activities. We can categorize businesses into three main types:

 a) <u>Service Companies:</u> These businesses provide services to meet customers' needs. Services can encompass various fields and may involve intangible assets such as knowledge and expertise. Examples include hotels, restaurants, legal firms, accounting services, coaching, and tutoring.
 b) <u>Industrial or Manufacturing Companies:</u> These are involved in transforming raw materials into finished products that are either sold directly to consumers or used as inputs by other companies. For instance, sawmills turn logs into wooden products.
 c) <u>Commercial Companies:</u> These companies act as intermediaries between manufacturers or other distributors and end consumers. They buy goods and

resell them. Examples include supermarkets, retail stores, and online marketplaces.

It's important to note that your choice of business type will impact the resources required, such as material, technology, human resources, and finances. Your decision should align with your skills, habits, and interests.

Choosing Your Business Idea

Now that you have a clearer understanding of business types, let's focus on selecting the specific business idea that suits you. Start by brainstorming and listing down all the business ideas that come to mind. Here's a step-by-step guide:

1. <u>Brainstorm:</u> Take a pen and paper and jot down every business idea that comes to mind. Don't censor your thoughts; write down everything.
2. <u>Analyze Your Ideas:</u> Once you have a list of ideas, analyze each one based on the following criteria: *Passion,* Choose an idea that genuinely excites you and aligns with your interests; *Innovation,* Seek unique and innovative ideas that add value to your product or service; *Profitability,* Evaluate the income potential of each idea. It should cover costs and generate profits.
3. <u>Problem-Solving:</u> Consider identifying common problems and finding innovative solutions to them. Solving everyday problems in a unique and efficient way can lead to successful entrepreneurship.
4. <u>Utilize Your Expertise:</u> If you have expertise or skills in a specific area, leverage them to develop a business

idea. Your unique perspective can offer a competitive advantage.
5. <u>Market Research:</u> Conduct interviews, surveys, or questionnaires to understand what potential customers need and how they prefer to have their needs met.
6. <u>Resource Assessment:</u> Consider the resources required for each idea and assess their availability. Remember that time is a valuable resource, and in some cases, you can start with limited capital and invest your time to gradually grow the business.
7. <u>Start Small and Grow:</u> You don't always need significant capital to start a business. Begin with what you have and reinvest your earnings to improve and expand over time.

Business Model Canvas

To further analyze and refine your business idea, you can use the Business Model Canvas, a tool developed by Yves Pigneur and Alexander Osterwalder. It helps define and visualize key components of your business model. The Canvas consists of nine parts: (See Figure No. 2).

1. <u>Value Proposition:</u> Define what unique value your business offers to customers.
2. <u>Customer Relationships:</u> Describe how you will engage and interact with customers.
3. <u>Channels:</u> Outline the strategies and channels for delivering your value proposition.
4. <u>Key Partners:</u> Identify strategic alliances, suppliers, and distributors that can enhance your business.

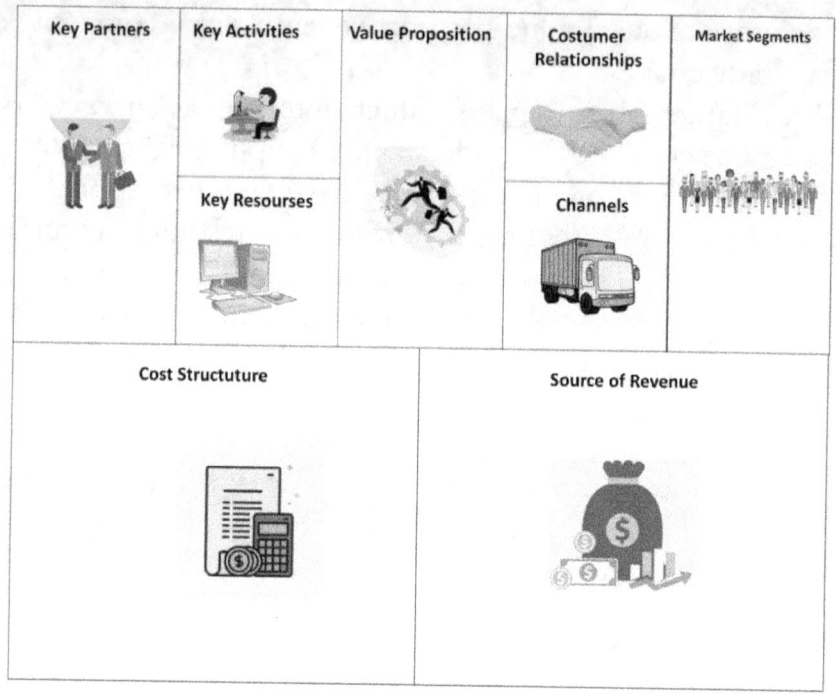

Figure No. 2. Canvas Model

5. <u>Market Segments:</u> Identify your target customers.
6. <u>Key Activities:</u> List essential activities required to deliver your value proposition.
7. <u>Key Resources:</u> Specify the resources necessary for your business operations.
8. <u>Cost Structure:</u> Analyze your business costs to ensure profitability.
9. <u>Sources of Revenue:</u> Determine how your business will generate income.

The Canvas Model helps you develop a comprehensive understanding of your business and its potential for success.

Leveraging Business Experts

Seeking guidance from experienced individuals can be invaluable on your entrepreneurial journey. Experts and mentors can provide:

- Networking: They can help you connect with relevant contacts and sources of financing.

- Support: Frequent mentoring sessions can provide guidance, accelerate learning, and offer solutions to problems.

- Objective Insights: Experts can provide objective perspectives and advice.

- Visualization: They can help you envision the lifestyle and work routine of a successful entrepreneur.

- Industry Knowledge: Experts in your field can offer insights specific to your industry.

Remember that mentors don't make decisions for you but guide you based on their experiences. Gradually, you'll become more self-reliant in making informed decisions. In contrast to mentors, coaches may not have expertise in your specific field but use tools and techniques to guide you towards achieving your goals.

Choosing a profitable business involves careful consideration of your interests, innovative ideas, and profitability potential. Use tools like the Business Model Canvas to refine your business concept. Seek guidance from experts and mentors to enhance your entrepreneurial journey. Remember that entrepreneurship is a learning process, so stay consistent and keep moving forward. Your vision and determination will guide you toward success in the business world.

CHAPTER V: Choose a Business That Gets You Closer to Your Dreams

Now that you've assessed your skills, interests, and chosen a business idea, it's crucial to ask yourself if this venture will bring you closer to your dreams. Entrepreneurship should be a path that leads you to a more fulfilling and satisfying life. Let's explore how to align your business with your dreams and work towards achieving them.

Defining Your Dreams

To start, you need to clearly define your dreams. Your dreams represent the things that bring you the most satisfaction and fulfillment in life. They could be related to various aspects, such as:

- Financial goals (e.g., earning a specific income, becoming financially independent).
- Lifestyle choices (e.g., living in a particular location, traveling the world, enjoying a certain quality of life).
- Personal aspirations (e.g., fame, power, making a positive impact on society).
- Unique experiences (e.g., exploring different cultures, conserving wildlife).

Once you've identified your dreams, it's essential to quantify them and set specific, measurable goals. This turns your dreams into achievable objectives that you can work towards.

Aligning Your Business with Your Dreams

Now, consider how your chosen business can help you move closer to your dreams. Entrepreneurship often serves three primary purposes:

1. <u>Generating Passive Income:</u> Your business should ideally become a source of passive income, meaning it generates revenue without requiring your continuous presence. This allows you to have more time and freedom to pursue your dreams.
2. <u>Meeting a Unique Need:</u> Your business should address a unique need in the market, setting it apart from competitors. This can lead to higher demand and profitability, providing you with resources to work toward your dreams.
3. <u>Creating Jobs:</u> By establishing and growing your business, you not only benefit yourself but also contribute to the economy by creating jobs for others.

Example Scenario: Culinary Business and World Travel Dream

Let's illustrate this concept with a hypothetical example: You've decided to enter the culinary business because you're skilled and passionate about cooking. However, your dream isn't to become a renowned chef or run a large restaurant. Instead, you dream of living on the sea, traveling the world, experiencing diverse cultures, foods, and interacting with different people.

Your culinary business can align with your dream in the following ways:

- Initially, your business may require substantial effort and time as most startups do. However, once it's established and can operate without your constant presence, you'll gain the freedom to travel.
- You can use your culinary skills and business to explore various cuisines and cultures around the world. Traveling to different places can enhance your culinary expertise and create unique experiences.

In this scenario, your business and dream are complementary. Your business provides the means and flexibility to achieve your dream of traveling the world while pursuing your culinary interests.

Achieving Your Dreams

To make progress toward your dreams, you must remain consistent and motivated. Here are some strategies to help you stay on track:

1. Focus on Your Dream: Concentrate on your dream itself, not the obstacles or how to get there. Visualize your dream as if you've already achieved it.
2. Document Your Dream: Write down your dream, define it, and turn it into a project. Create a tangible portfolio or folder labeled with your dream's name to signify your commitment to achieving it.
3. Share Your Dream: Share your dream with your close circle, seeking not just approval but also valuable

contacts and potential partners who can assist you in your journey.
4. <u>Persistence is Key:</u> Understand that persistence often matters more than opportunity. Rejections and setbacks are part of the process. See them as "not right now" rather than "never."
5. <u>Set Smaller Goals:</u> If circumstances or setbacks slow your progress, set smaller, achievable goals to maintain forward momentum.
6. <u>Help Others:</u> Provide support and assistance to others when you can. Helping others can open doors, create valuable connections, and bring unexpected opportunities.

Remember that achieving your dreams is a journey, not just a destination. Stay committed, remain persistent, and continue dreaming. Your entrepreneurial endeavors should serve as a vehicle to bring you closer to your dreams and create a more fulfilling life.

CONCLUSIONS

In conclusion, the entrepreneurial journey is a path filled with decisions, challenges, and opportunities for growth and success. This book has provided insights into how to choose a business idea that aligns with your skills, interests, and personal characteristics, emphasizing the importance of self-awareness and careful consideration.

In today's competitive landscape, entrepreneurship has become a popular choice for many individuals, whether in the digital realm or traditional brick-and-mortar businesses. The decision to embark on this journey is significant, and selecting the right business idea is a crucial step. It's important to remember that patience and dedication are essential, and the time and effort you invest in your business are valuable, even if you don't have access to substantial capital.

Keep in mind that there are no insurmountable obstacles, only challenges that require time and effort to overcome. Rejection should be seen as a temporary setback, and maintaining persistence is key. Sharing your dreams with your inner circle can lead to valuable contacts and help keep your motivation high. To turn your dreams into reality, it's essential to focus on them and transform them into actionable projects. Dedication and persistence are fundamental to achieving success. Instead of being discouraged by obstacles, seek ways to overcome them, and break your journey into smaller, achievable goals to maintain forward momentum.

Additionally, consider the power of helping others whenever you have the opportunity. Not only is it rewarding, but it can also open unexpected doors on your path toward realizing your dreams.

Always remember that change is constant in the world of entrepreneurship, and your endeavors have the potential to make a significant impact by addressing needs, creating jobs, and contributing to the growth of your community and country. Continue your journey toward your dreams with determination and never give up.

I appreciate your interest in this book, and I encourage you to share your feedback on the platform where you obtained it and on our social media channels. If you wish to explore specific topics further or require additional guidance, please don't hesitate to reach out. Together, we can enrich our knowledge and make progress toward our entrepreneurial goals. Wishing you tremendous success on your path to achieving your dreams!

ABOUT THE AUTHOR

Carlos Cárdenas Verde graduated in Public Accounting from Universidad Nacional Experimental de los Llanos Ezequiel Zamora, Barinas, Venezuela in 2000. With extensive experience as an accountant, financial advisor, and business management consultant, Carlos has devoted much of his career to educating both young people and adults in educational institutions such as the Instituto Universitario de Tecnología Coronel Agustín Codazzi and the Universidad Nacional Experimental Simón Rodríguez.

In addition to his teaching experience, Carlos is recognized for his focus on developing valuable tools for accounting and management information within companies. Through self-taught learning in Digital Marketing and Digital Entrepreneurship, Carlos advocates for teaching accounting as a fundamental pillar for business success and entrepreneurship.

www.ingramcontent.com/pod-product-compliance
Lightning Source LLC
Chambersburg PA
CBHW072050230526
45479CB00009B/337